Taking Cerebral Palsy To School

JayJo Books, L.L.C.
Publishing Special Books for Special Kids ®
P.O. Box 213
Valley Park, MO 63088-0213

Published by
JayJo Books, L.L.C.
P.O. Box 213
Valley Park, MO 63088-0213

Edited by Kim Gosselin

Library of Congress Cataloging-In-Publication Data
Anderson, Mary Elizabeth
Taking Cerebral Palsy to School/Mary Elizabeth Anderson-First Edition
Library of Congress Catalog Card Number 00-190096
1.Children's Disabilities
2.School Mainstreaming
3.Children's Literature

ISBN 1-891383-08-6
Library of Congress
6th book in our *"Special Kids in School"*® series.

*All books printed by JayJo Books, L.L.C. are available at special quantity discounts when purchased in bulk. Special imprints, logos, messages and excerpts can be designed to meet your needs. For more information call the publisher at 636-861-1331 or fax at 636-861-2411. E-mail us at jayjobooks@aol.com.

Dedication

This book is dedicated to all children
who teach us about differences and similarities,
but especially to Chad Madson and his family
from Lincoln, Nebraska

A Note from the Author:

As a mother of two children born with congenital health defects, (one with a heart problem and the other born with Tracheoesophageal Fistula), I am always interested in seeking information that can educate others regarding health concerns.

Fortunately, my two children's conditions were corrected surgically at an early age. However, during my long stays at the University of Iowa hospital, I became acquainted with many children and parents who would have to live long-term, with chronic conditions and/or special needs.

Taking Cerebral Palsy to School was written after meeting a special boy, Chad Madson. Together with his parents, Craig and Connie, and his sister Marty, their compassion and knowledge regarding cerebral palsy was astounding and truly impressed me. It is my goal for Taking Cerebral Palsy to School to educate parents, teachers, friends, and caregivers regarding the special needs of children living with cerebral palsy.

Mary Elizabeth Anderson

Hello boys and girls! My name is Chad and I'm a kid living with cerebral palsy, or "CP" for short. I was born with cerebral palsy. Most kids living with CP were born with it, too. Sometimes though, boys and girls can get cerebral palsy later in life (maybe because of an accident). Kids who get CP later, are usually pretty young; often less than two years old.

Some kids living with cerebral palsy can do lots and lots of things. Other kids can't do as much. Remember, everyone is different. Even kids living with CP!

Having cerebral palsy means my brain has been hurt or injured in some way. A small part of my brain gets mixed-up messages. Because of this, it's usually hard for me to control my muscles. They are very weak.

There are three different kinds of CP. I have a little bit of all three. The most important thing I want you to understand about cerebral palsy is, that it's not a disease!

Living with cerebral palsy makes me work extra hard to try to get my muscles to do what I want them to do. I have to think extra hard whenever I want to talk, comb my hair, or even hold a cup of milk.

Luckily though, someone called a "physical therapist" works with me to help make my muscles stronger. He helps make it easier for me to do "everyday" things.

My leg muscles are very weak. That makes it hard for me to move them. It helps a lot if I use a wheelchair. Sometimes though, I can walk with leg braces.

Leg braces help to stretch the muscles in my legs to make them stronger. That's good!

Sometimes, when I'm wearing my leg braces, I might feel like taking them off. That's okay. Especially if I want to go swimming. I love to swim with my dad.

Swimming is an exercise that helps my legs get stronger!

Would you like to know what living with cerebral palsy might feel like? When you get home, try putting three socks on your hands. Then try to button or unbutton your shirt or blouse. It won't be easy!

That's kind of what I feel like, living with cerebral palsy. It isn't easy.

Just like you, I go to school almost every day. Lots of kids living with CP go to regular public schools. Like any kid, some may go to private schools or study at home.

When I go to school, I get to ride a school bus that has a special elevator in it. It's fun! It lifts me and my wheelchair up onto the bus.

I really like to learn new things at school. It's fun to play with my friends, too. I like all of my teachers and my physical therapist, too. They all help me to say new sounds, speak new words, and learn new exercises!

The exercises help my arms and legs grow much stronger! My teachers and physical therapist help me in so many different ways. I feel really lucky to have them!

At times, I may have trouble making sounds or talking. You might not be able to understand me all of the time. Remember, it's really hard for me to get the words out exactly right. The muscles in my mouth and throat are very weak. I might say some words really slow. Some of my words might even sound funny to you!

Talking "funny" doesn't mean I'm stupid, though! In fact, I'm very smart!!

A lot of kids living with cerebral palsy (like me) have to wear something on their heads called "headgear". My headgear might look strange to you, but it helps protect my head in case I have a seizure and fall. It's kind of like the helmet you wear when you ride a bike!

A seizure is kind of hard to explain. Seizures can happen when the messages going to my brain get all mixed up. Having a seizure can make my body shake really hard. This can make me fall down or fall out of my wheelchair.

Seizures aren't anything for you to be afraid of. They usually don't last long or happen very often. Besides, my headgear helps to keep me safe!

Don't worry, you can't catch cerebral palsy (or seizures) from me or anyone else! So, it's okay to play with me and be my friend. Everyone needs to have friends!

When you see someone in a wheel chair (like me), don't be afraid! Stop by and say "hi". It really makes me (and anyone else in a wheelchair) feel really GOOD!

Right now, there isn't a cure for cerebral palsy. That means my doctors and nurses can't "make it go away". But, my whole family, together with my doctors, nurses, and physical therapist help me to "manage" it in the best way possible.

I'm learning how to control my muscles better and better everyday, too. Soon, I may be able to do more and more for myself!

Living with cerebral palsy is really just a very small part of who I am. In every other way, I'm just like you!

THE END

LET'S TAKE THE CEREBRAL PALSY KIDS QUIZ!

1. **Does living with cerebral palsy mean you're "sick"?**
   No, getting a cold would make me sick. Cerebral palsy is just part of who I am.

2. **Do you ever feel sad because you live with cerebral palsy?**
   Sometimes, I guess. Especially when kids don't understand. They might act like I don't even exist! That can really hurt my feelings and make me feel sad.

3. **Will you ever get better?**
   Remember, cerebral palsy can't be cured. But, there are a lot of good ways to help manage it. There are some things I won't ever be able to do, but that's true for everyone!

4. **What part of your body causes you to have a seizure sometimes?**
   My brain. Sometimes, it gets mixed up messages.

5. **Can I catch cerebral palsy from you?**
   No, it's not contagious! It's okay to play with me and be my friend. I can't give you CP.

6. **Did you do anything wrong to cause your CP?**
   No, cerebral palsy is just something that "happened" to me.

7. **Do you want to be treated any differently because you live with cerebral palsy?**
   Never! Just try to be patient with me and understanding. On the inside, I'm a lot like everyone else. I have feelings, too!

8. **What does a physical therapist do?**
   A physical therapist helps me to use my muscles better. They help me do exercises to make my muscles get stronger.

9. **Because you live with cerebral palsy, do other kids ever make fun of you or call you names?**
   Yes, and that hurts my feelings. But, I think kids do things like that because they really don't understand what cerebral palsy is. Now, hopefully you understand it better!

10. **Do you like to have friends and play sports?**
   Sure I do. Doesn't everyone? Sometimes, I might need help playing certain kinds of sports, though. My favorite sports are horseback riding and swimming!

Great Job! Thanks for taking the Cerebral Palsy Kid's Quiz, and learning more about CP!

TEN TIPS FOR TEACHERS

✓ **1. MANY CHILDREN WITH CEREBRAL PALSY ARE MENTALLY SOUND.**
Be extra sensitive to their needs. Sometimes, it embarrasses children living with cerebral palsy to eat in the regular lunchroom since they may wear a special bib and use a special cup. Try to find out how they feel about it before you make a decision.

✓ **2. CHILDREN LIVING WITH CEREBRAL PALSY USUALLY CANNOT BEGIN TO PHYSICALLY KEEP UP WITH OTHER STUDENTS.**
Please be patient and take time to modify their schoolwork. For example: If all students are asked to write 25 sentences, ask your CP student to write 5.

✓ **3. MANY TEACHERS MISTAKENLY THINK IT WORKS BEST TO PUT CP CHILDREN IN THE FRONT OF THE ROOM.**
Sitting so close to the audio-visual equipment may hurt their necks. It might be best to have them sit in the middle of the room.

✓ **4. GET THE CP STUDENT INVOLVED WITH STRONG ROLE MODEL KIDS.**
Kids with strong role models know CP children need special attention and they will give it to them. This gives both of the students extra confidence!

✓ **5. MAKE SURE YOUR CP STUDENT HAS AN IMPORTANT PART IN SCHOOL MUSIC PROGRAMS OR PLAYS.**
Make the CP student a significant part of special programs so he or she will receive positive recognition. For example: If a program takes place at Christmas time, let your CP student play the part of Santa. The wheelchair could work as Santa's sleigh.
Be creative and you will be rewarded!

6. TEACHERS NEED TO INCLUDE CP CHILDREN IN SPORTS ACTIVITIES.
Try to create special adaptations for these children. Most of them love sports! Let these kids try to hit the ball with their hand, kick it with their leg, or try some other creative experiment. You'll win a smile everytime!

7. THE BATHROOM CAN CREATE A PROBLEM FOR CP CHILDREN.
If your CP student is mentally capable, he or she will probably be sensitive and self-conscious about this experience. Ask your student if he or she would like to use the facilities in a Special Education room. Let the student decide!

8. TRY TO FIND A SPECIAL ASSISTANT, AID, OR HELPER FOR THE CP STUDENT.
Since regular class work proves very demanding for children living with cerebral palsy, this is particularly important if they are totally mainstreamed into the classroom.

9. CHILDREN WITHOUT CP WONDER ABOUT SPECIFIC SIGNS, LIKE THE STICK MAN SITTING IN A WHEELCHAIR.
When students ask about this, simply explain it is a symbol for "handicap". It has the same meaning all around the world!

10. CHILDREN WITHOUT CP MAY ASK YOU WHY SOME PEOPLE GET CEREBRAL PALSY AND OTHERS DON'T.
Explain that cerebral palsy "just happens". The best message you can teach your students is that we all need to accept each person's strong points and weak points. We should always celebrate what we **CAN** do!!

To order additional copies of <u>Taking Cerebral Palsy to School</u> contact your local bookstore or library, or call the publisher directly at 1-(636) 861-1331. Visit our website at: **www.jayjo.com.** E-mail us at: **jayjobooks@aol.com.**

Write to us at:
JayJo Books, L.L.C.
P.O. Box 213
Valley Park, MO 63088-0213

LOOK FOR OTHER BOOKS IN OUR
SPECIAL KIDS IN SCHOOL® **SERIES,**
INCLUDING:
<u>Taking Diabetes to School</u>
<u>Taking Asthma to School</u>
<u>Taking Seizure Disorders to School</u>
<u>Taking Food Allergies to School</u>
<u>Taking A.D.D. to School</u>
<u>Taking Cystic Fibrosis to School</u>
And others coming soon!

Others Available Now!
<u>SPORTSercise!</u>
A "School" Story About Exercise-Induced Asthma
<u>Taking Asthma to Camp</u>
A Fictional Story About Asthma Camp
<u>ZooAllergy</u>
A Fun Story About Allergy and Asthma Triggers
<u>Rufus Comes Home</u>
Rufus The Bear With Diabetes™
A Fictional Story about the Diagnosis of Diabetes
<u>The ABC's of Asthma</u>
An Asthma Alphabet Book for Kids of All Ages

<u>Taming the Diabetes Dragon</u>
A Fictional Story About Learning to Live Better with Diabetes
<u>Trick-or-Treat for Diabetes</u>
A Halloween Story for Kids Living with Diabetes

And our first large hardcover book:
<u>Smoking STINKS!!®</u>
from our new *Substance Free Kids*® series.

A portion of the proceeds from all our publications is donated to various charities to help fund important medical research and education. We work hard to make a difference in the lives of children with chronic conditions and/or special needs. Thank you for your support.